Larger Than Blue

J. FRYBERGER VOTE

To Dana & Richard

Love,

Jeanne

Published through Opus Self-Publishing Services
Located at:
Politics and Prose Bookstore
5015 Connecticut Ave. NW
Washington, D.C. 20008
www.politics-prose.com / / (202) 364-1919

Notes

In this set of selected and new poems you will find a variety of form and structure, driven by content. Time and space links as in "concurrencies," diverse perspectives of beauty, and the significance of a tiny moment (poetry as a microscope) interest me. Being a musician who learned to read notes before words, I am keenly aware of rhythm, the sounds of internal rhyme, and the clicking of hard consonants. Some pieces are intended to be read at a fast tempo as in "Nine Days in Nice," or "Nectarine Cornbread." Poems like "Raposa" are more relaxed and contemplative with chantlike repetition. Understated playful sarcasm is evident in "Redundancies" with phrases that spiral back into themselves.

There are many people who have contributed to my continuing attempt to poet. I am deeply grateful to Lucille Clifton for many years of mentoring and irreverent laughter. To the friends, sisters, and writers who encouraged me, I am aware of your gift. My husband, Larry, is my constant. He is my reader, serious support, and understands my occasional bouts of obsessive focus. It is solo work. Both seekers of art, we are a devoted team.

Born in a small town in Washington State, living many years in rural Maryland, I now enjoy daily access to a myriad of D.C. urban enrichments. The big windowed light from my 4th floor condo makes the world seem *larger than blue.*

JFV

Contents

Counterpoint

Wandering

Kith and Kin

COUNTERPOINT

Cable Car Rise

A glass box
lifts effortlessly
silently
an elegant arc
over the crane
delicately placing
triangle struts
above the tallest
vanilla pine
beyond granite
into thinner air
accelerating
strange visions
Henry Moore
gone wild
then at the edge
of the earth
a lake appears
larger than blue
letting go
lifting us still
into a Kandinsky
sky.

Redundancies

Experimental poetry. Irish depression medication.
Love never ends. Ends are always beginnings.
Church music. Mother Theresa's compassion.
Escape by television. Work exhaustion.
Cultural awareness. Complicated family reunions.
Rain releases tension. Cinnamon and morning.
Performance anxiety. Dance movement.
Binge thinking. Pure random form and nature.

The Button

Once while working
a button dropped off my blouse.

I asked the kind woman
in the office next to mine

if she had a pin
or a needle and thread.

Sitting in the light
of her window

for an unexpected
vintage moment

still wearing the
broken top, she

gently and expertly
sewed it back on

my breath   suspended
in simple intimacy.

Amadou

Policemen cried white tears
in living color, on the evening news
after pumping 41 bullets, 19
into your black wallet body.
Bending over, they whispered
"Don't die, please don't die."
But you laid still, your doorway
punctured with error.
No public remorse can alter
this red river flowing from
holes in judgement.

Kadiatou, mother
your sweet round face
mirrors his, shy hope of justice
from a larger tyranny.
The new land, freedom
failed you. As you gently
bow to Mecca five times this day
what do you ask?
The world sees the elephant
in the center of the courtroom
but the jury does not.

New York City
1999

Tribute to a Teacher

Lucille

your gray locks glow

holding thoughts

said and unsaid.

Egos surround you

but you are unaffected.

Calm soft beauty

you don't need

clever placement

of borrowed phrases

or draped hair

skimming bare breasts.

You have known passion.

Now you speak

the language

for us.

Geraldine R. Dodge Poetry Festival

Beach

There are infinite colors of blue:
Atlantic, Caribbean, Pacific,
Mediterranean, Adriatic....

Clouds exist as a reflection
of a breaking wave
one with gravity, the other weightless.

Shorelines are the border between
imagination and action.
They are constantly overlapping.

The invisible moon adds force,
a comforting repetition
the sun, desire.

Miso Kale

Winter moon rising
Unknown to us

Maintaining clean lives
Under laundromat light strips

Familiar task shared
With random strangers

Language barriers excluded
Downtown mix

Elegant historic hotels
Turned condo

Dancers, too thin
Homemade street pizza

Around the corner
A dark shoe repair shop

Spicy thick scent
He fixes a singer's boots

Her favorite
Yes, it matters

City time together
Quiet Saturday morning

Miso kale
For breakfast.

Bread of Tears ✓

"You have fed them with the bread of tears;
you have given them bowls of tears to drink" from psalm 80

Long after the weeping and rocking
ends, death remains.

Holes the size of fear
carved into pieces of family
sewn together with love
interrupted by memory.

Hallway portrait
four plates on the table
instead of five, voice missing
the unspoken name.

Why the lambs?

I want to be a mender
silver needle allowed inside
particularly sharp
delicately binding strength.

I want to bake sweet cakes
pour warm milk and honey
over despair, be a
shepherd of sorrow.

Noticing

Walking into the woods
the field guides stop
by a 300-year-old Jeffrey Pine.

He sets up the long lens
to see a golden eagle
while she gently
opens the wings
of a grasshopper
exposing delicate etchings.

While she is talking
he carefully picks a bug
off her bare arm
with extreme tenderness

a piece of sky

wings hard to decipher
strong wire-like veins
move deftly into uncomfortable spaces
no attention drawn

surrounding architecture begins to shift
crashing dangerously
edges of perception, threatened
every familiar path implodes

still, momentum persists
darting in many directions at once
appearing daily to the mess
singing towards unnamed light

small packages of moonglow
reflect affection, possibility
in one, a star
a piece of sky opens

Grounded

This is a strong tree, low voiced

Reassuring

Branches curl around family first

Protecting and expanding

Then students, strangers, friends

This thirsty planet

Human words perfectly placed

To feed a mysterious life

One that connects us

Artistic roots

Throwing shade at fear

Gathering complexity, each cycle

Losing leaves, providing

Space for new light

Sago Mine Disaster

Stretched out face down
peering between the plastic strips
of a white Caribbean beach chair
I see pieces of broken shell
and crystal sand sparkling
arranging themselves in text
telling stories of the twelve
miners far below the surface
of the same earth, who today
were discovered dead.

From another world we watch
the white egret of resurrection
pass before us
its coal black legs carefully
placing each step
to gobble up unsuspecting parts
in the family of things.

Slow steady rhythm of equatorial waters
does not calm waves of uncommon grief.
Even the Full Body Evangelical
Pentecostal Church where they gathered
could not contain the anger.

It burst into our room-with-a-view
as the news caught the same sunrise
the same sun we try to block
to keep the burn of loss away.

2006

The strength of this poem

depends on the ability

to eliminate words

unnecessary

to the

message.

three potatoes

early morning dew
slug trails and spider webs
sparkle, until humans
break the spell

a steel garden tool
slices the earth
and without knowing, a worm
my hands curve gently underneath
lifting out one, two, three potatoes

umbilical vines disconnected
i rinse dirt off the triplets
and my fingernails
to find how exquisite
common can be

voluptuous brown curves
the white insides heavy
with moist nutrients
enough to sustain my Irish roots
for centuries

blessed by the gods
a fertile place for growth
i will make soup
to share with friends
three toes in a pot

Vanishing Point

There is a point
at which one
can become invisible
absent of presence
in order to survive.

Maybe this space is safe
a resting place for power
the sort that others
do not recognize, but
but like a magnetic field
holds everything in balance.

Maybe this space is risk
to face an ordinary day
addicted to sadness, fearful
someone will notice
neutral empty eyes.

Open wounds of the spirit
waiting to be tended,
there is a point
of no return.

Five Empty Chairs

Part I

At the edge of the lawn
facing the river, sit five
empty Adirondack chairs
slightly curved inward
a ghostly conversation.

Red chrysanthemums
in weathered barrel pots
guard the dock
uniformed sentinels.

Gone are the noisy ski boats
rising in steep acceleration
anticipating
the thrill and the fall equally
then circling back
scent of sun lotion and beer.

Gone are the monster yachts
that anchor
and claim the sunset
as their own private story.

Gone are the tiny wave runners
darting across the water

angry weighted dragonflies
sans iridescent wings.

Part II

Now only the silent kayaks
slip into the inlet
reverent trespassers of the marsh
pausing in the center
to listen and drift.

Several white egrets
approve of their visit, remain still
while a small junco
circles twice
sounding the warning.

Six big blues
time reversed pterodactyls
suddenly rise
shaking periwinkles
clinging to tall grass.

Soon the cold will bring
early morning oystermen
harvesting
ancient beds that sleep
crackly shells and barnacles.

Beginning of a Poem

Mom, the poison ivy
You removed from my front yard
Without my knowing
Is growing back

Nectarine Cornbread

in the voice of Sarah Palin, a nasal fast self-assured northern drawl

I was warming up lasagna in the oven when
it became clear that Todd might be a little tired
this being the third day in a row, but ya know
what can he expect when I am on the stump
with the mouths of Track, Bristol, Willow, Piper
and Trig to feed. The hungry press is watching
for the wide-eyed Alaskan governor to trip…
(wow, great name for our next child) while
bringing home the bacon and cooking it up.

So, there were some nectarines left over
from the fruit salad a few weeks ago
and I just threw them in the blender
with nutmeg, and an extra egg for protein
when you don't have venison or rabbit.
It was the color of rich gold, just like it had
been panned up-country, then I sliced some
mortgage lifter tomatoes to contrast the
corn sweetness leaning toward soft politics.

river ✓

the river in her
runs constantly
burbling forward

the river is rich
with blueberry fields
of sheep

there are three paths
to the river
all are true

all lead to the sea

The Organ Builder and the Organist

Your highly trained hands carefully lift the front panel
exposing the complicated system of community inside.
It is not physically easy to do.
You must bend, your body rebelling
to see into the layered array of connecting rods
deployed by my hands and feet.

Thirty years, I have pressed the keys into active duty
sometimes reaching a warm embrace,
stories of lost loved ones melt in hidden emotion
other times rejoicing in the sheer power
that pipes joined with a reckless diversity of voices
pour forth from wooden pews.

I wonder who put me in this driver's seat
this bench between heaven and earth.
The act of engaging the strength of ancient tunes
composed and sung by ancestors,
courage to taste the dangerous hymn
slightly dissonant or rhythmically uneven

would render useless a quiet bird,
an introvert observing particular gifts each Sunday.
Glass shades open with a foot pedal
controlling just how much music will be set free.
Perhaps the organ builder is here to unlock
a mysterious new set of sounds

that have not been heard in this space.
He struggles to patiently remove
each existing handmade worn-out part
disintegrating before our eyes, a slow process
relative to the importance of the next
sacred code resonating curiosity and history.

hurricane

cornerstones of a promise
this boat, ingeniously tied
suspended
between four strong pilings
from harm and from safety

ropes are all that remain

Airport Reunion

Two children peer down the long jetway.
Many strangers walk by, then he appears.
They are scooped up, giant arms pressing
midnight feeding, first steps, Irish curls
into his chest forever.
Blood secrets of time passing.

A stolen tryst.

She is watching as he opens his eyes.
No sensual touch could equal this gaze,
this full pause of spirit recognition.
Family made whole by the only human
in the universe that knows everything
and expects nothing of this moment.

Old Soul

I cannot claim
any insight
I might have

or the angst
that sometimes
clouds
my vision.

I am
a composite
of all
that came
before.

Blue Neon Halo

The night air is still
only eyelids
       open and close
       open and close.

Tears collect in corners
drop on the pillow
       silently stinging
       silently stinging.

Voices of sadness
invade then implode
       nobody knows
       nobody knows.

A cold sheet of glass
"touch me I'll shatter"
       pieces won't fit
       pieces won't fit.

During the day
numbness is painful
       shielding distress
       shielding distress.

A blue neon halo
is all she will earn
       desperate courage
       desperate courage.

Rest Home Ritual

Since birds are lifted
by their wings
it is fitting
this final sign
in the long gray hall
an earthly ornament
exquisite, unique
still
like each person
asleep, behind doors
marked at the top
with a single feather
falling
at the morning opening.

Today
one remains,
bold blue pattern
horizontal black stripes
delicate white tips
a songbird.
Whose daughter, sister
whose life
will change forever
gentle passing
spirit from body
to another place

no halls, no doors
what kind of beauty
this crossing?

Stepping Over

For many years
in the part of my life
as a kindergarten teacher
there was a day
that I stepped over reason
to become Mary Poppins.

It was an easy transformation.
I secretly believed
all my educational pedagogy
could be reduced to
removing fear, and
encouraging imagination.

So, every Halloween
I grabbed my carpet bag
and brally
put on my flowered hat
and marched through the school
with 28 Michaels and Janes
singing, "Just a Spoonful…"

At lunch we made the whole
cafeteria guilty,
singing "Feed the Birds."
After drawing chalk pictures
on the playground
I put them to rest with
"Stay Awake, Don't Go to Sleep."

Dance Music

The silent pianist sits invisible
providing musical space in which to move.
Parallel activity.

Suddenly, an energy exchange
source obscured   embraces
perfectly controlled body rhythms.

In absence of ego
dance and music flow effortlessly
transcending abilities.

Later,
eyes of dancers and pianist connect.

They know
the relentless hours
are for these moments.

Woman with a Bag of Basil

She walked away
leaving a trail of scent
invisible green cloud
lifting from a plain brown bag
in a hurry, her quick steps
cracking a stone rhythm
purposeful - forward momentum
would she cut tiny strips
to cook over open flame
hidden deep in a reduced sauce
or place carefully
on bright red roma tomatoes
plump as her parted lips
sparkling, olive oil golden.

                White dew-
one drop
                on each thorn.

By Yosa Buson, from *The Essential Haiku,* by Robert Haas

to the muse

small voices move me most
slow singing, unaccompanied
basket of poems by the door
sparkling insect wing
clean high-country breeze
stray columbine in a rock garden
blackberry thorn sting
bare toes in a cold stream

next time i get lost
in worldly obedience
false gods preying
on my tired uneasy soul
send me a sign
to return
and i will listen
one healing drop at a time

WANDERING

FRANCE

Nine Days in Nice

At breakfast the tart leaned over gently
and picked a white raisin from the tan arm
of the airline pilot who was not impressed
with chocolate croissants brought to him by
someone with "Just Do It" written
on the back of her pants. He did not recognize
delight in the shape of a morning coffee.

Boardwalk skaters skim easily
above drunk white drummers in a circle
warm from the day of comfortable bodies
soaking up vitamins and cancer at the same rate
while default ashtrays hug every cocktail table.
Rubber ankles crisscross red beer cup obstacles so fast
you might not notice the smell of crepes being grilled
in the soft air or the very real possibility
of stepping into a Mary Poppins painting.

When a person dressed in a formal and stilettos
whizzed by too close on a cobalt blue motor scooter
I was in the middle of a ham and cheese sandwich
but I didn't mind because the bread was so soft inside
the crust hard like beach rocks, then a dip
and the piercing French pipes of the great organ
like my dangling legs, sounded a sudden cold shock
but were buoyed up by saltwater.
Even though the swell was far above my head

I could not be afraid of the carnival
surrounding the enormous cathedral silence.

Shaking from an unmentioned disease
the Franciscan monk in common clothes
with Mediterranean blue eyes sparkling in late sun
giggled when we learned in broken half-language
that he was a professor of Greek, but
he thought being a professor of music
must surely be better. He walked us to the small
open window and pointed at the cast iron
crossed arms, a hole in each hand
on the top of the monastery, then turned
to shake our whole-less hands.

Four women as old as the olive trees that shaded them
were having a beer while discussing politics
and children alternately. The one with long white hair
pulled up with an ornamented clip
was the mother of Matisse. She was saying
that Henri was a fool to quit being a law clerk in Paris
and he never went to mass since. Sitting to the left,
the friend with too much gold jewelry said that
designing the chapel for the Dominicans probably
saved him from hell, and think of how much you can get
for a chair he sat in once, and they all laughed.

Terrified at the possibility of even one meal without dessert
we walked past the coiffure with the old-fashioned domed hair dryers,
two mysterious people in white near the door of the clinique,
fresh fruit, rotisserie chicken, a window of candy,
a small dog of a matched set peeing on the church steps
unknown to its oblivious owner walking ahead,
another coiffure and then the patisserie. We greedily eyed
every chocolate pastry or sweet piece of material culture there.
She didn't have to carefully box and wrap our simple choice
in yellow paper with yellow ribbon
but how else would we find our way home?

A motorcyclist in full black leather gear
with a pointed steel wrist band
is doing tai chi in the middle of the market
when the two-toned siren begins and oh my god,
perfect fruits and vegetables are flying through the air
into the window of the very fancy gift shop
where nothing is useful but everything is beautiful
and people red as lobsters, are running
to save the lamps made of gourds from
being strangled by the leather and bead necklaces,
when the life-sized plaster of Paris chef
in front of the restaurant comes alive
and stops the chaos with one word – beach.
For your penance you must all go to the beach
and be pounded by the waves. Only then
will you be allowed to return to the disorder
of this grande civilization.

I wore my lemon and orange scarf to the ballet
and like a blended pina colada with an umbrella,
mixed with the glittering crowd of pointed-toed ladies
with too little flesh but more than enough excitement
for the red velvet opera house wrapped around the 18th century,
each box with mirrors that gave away secrets. In the middle
of the orchestra during the tango, the bandaneon man
put his foot on a chair and soared to a small back room
in Argentina, where we met in tears.

Roasted roquefort and pears
came to the table without permission.
They just appeared and of course,
we greeted them with wild abandon.
There was a warning of sweet onions and red mullet
and we knew that chocolate mousse was coming later,
but this was unexpected in the usual melon sequence
of early evening with its olive and martini visit
leaving us poised and ready for more.

Gallery Guard

I want to have that job
the person who sits in a chair
watching Picasso with one eye
gallery visitors observing the paintings with another
and with the third eye, a small window to the sea.

They rotate rooms
Miro is next and then downstairs
sacred works of Fra Angelico
so much detail on which to dwell
metaphysical language.

But also thinking, when his break comes
he would like that tuna sandwich with chives
and a crispy cold beer. Then perhaps a pass
by the music shop window to see
the violin he is wishing for his daughter.

The Clock Tower Bell

History still rings.

A fickle companion, Time.
When night compacts
anxieties into nightmares
Time is locked out.

Watching hot summer sun
ripen cherry tomatoes
from a soft garden bench
Time falls away, unfazed.

If it could only linger
like overtones floating
after the strike.

17th century Auvillar

Hotel Taureau

I listen without decoding
a conversation below
intuiting meaning.
Breeze gets stronger
shutters close out the storm
but not contradictions,
familiar strangers
serving each meal with grace
speak in expression only.

The skateboard hiding beneath
a magazine rack in the bar
means children. A family
business reflecting intentional
inclusion, annuals and perennials.
A boy brings a plate of haricot verts
to the table, his father the chef
watches every detail of his growth
without him knowing.

She appears, dark eyes and hair,
in a black dancing dress, shawl
pinned with a gold bull, hotel icon.
The mother is an evening star.
Proud of her family's constructed
lifestyle on a 17th century stage,
she welcomes international
travelers in their own language
borrowing their adventures.

Missing Home

Right now, on an island in the sea of restlessness
it is raining. Not a damaging rain. Sturdy
voluptuous drops that roll off the silver underside
of butterfly bush leaves. She is fiercely independent.

Why does it matter if the spider in the center of
the web is alone? Her heart beats twice the speed
of a sparrow. She climbs across exquisite geometry
and returns without slipping into temptation.

Why then, is the deep blue flag of emptiness flying
the edges irregular, like knots
in the lower regions of the stomach
where sadness collects.

She thinks longing is relative to desire. That the
clouds bringing rain have substance and purpose.
That waiting   listening   is indeed prologue.
Is loneliness an unwanted condition of freedom?

Guitar Man

Peering through a thin lace curtain
from my third-floor hotel desk
I see a person on the park bench below
playing guitar.
I can't hear him.

From the way he cradles the instrument
so familiar, intricate finger placement
it must be lovely music.

A white-haired man in a work shirt
sits relaxed, seemingly unaffected
on the next bench.

People pass in conversation
cars whiz by.

I open the window.

Slowly the invisible park musician
lowers the guitar into the case
looks up
lights a cigarette, and wonders
what I am writing.

Croissant

they woke

wrapped in buttery sheets

folded in a delicious spiral

sinking into softness

new summer morning light

filtered by tall white shutters

coffee and ocean

waiting

Hotel Aria

The wooden railing worn smooth
by generations of hands
is on the inside of the spiral staircase.
Narrow slivers of worn carpet
make the climb risky.

I opened the delicate ironwork elevator
lifted by gravity and cords only
saw the salmon red stained glass
at the landing, heard an amazing sound

and stepped into air.
The fall was short,
a slightly twisted ankle
the only consequence.

My happily distracted life is full of
near misses for the sake of beauty.

Strained muscles will heal
train schedules will pass, but the
stunning phrase in my daughter's aria
is still ringing in my head.

SPAIN

Clementine

A gift from Spain
bursts on my tongue
taste buds tingle
juices surround
orange
as afternoon sun
on hills, flowing
down
my grateful throat
little kisses
sweet proportion
centering senses
horizons
beyond this place.

ITALY

concurrencies ✓

white petals carry spring to us
my neighbor's wedding dress cherry
sprinkled over the back deck
by the same air that carries
morning scent
of chocolate and hazelnuts cooking
in alba
across big water
where white star jasmine
blossoms bursting
reflect the same moon

concomitanze

la primavera ci giunge
con i bianchi petali del ciliegio
del mio vicino di casa
sparsi sul patio come un abito da sposa
dalla stessa brezza
che ad Alba
si carica di cioccolato e nocciole
profumo del mattino
attraverso il grande fiume
dove i boccioli di gelsomino
fiorendo in bianche stele
riflettono la stessa luna

Italian translation by Dino Bosco

10 pm, Hotel Perpoin ✓

Handmade wooden shutters
strain soft balcony air

from my stiff clean sheets
I see a small lady in all black

fresh armful of red, blue, and green
walk toward a shrine

above, a young soprano repeats
the same Mozart passage, full voice

above that, a spiral brick chimney
looks at the moon, not quite full

below, a quartet rehearses
complex architectures, sound

spilling over the foundation
of medieval tiles not in museums

underground springs from the Alps
making floors wonderfully uneven

while a girl and her grandmother
eating gelato, look up

and see a warm light
in room 15.

Shopping with Pearls

You can step onto the balcony in slippers
wear garden sandals to pluck ripe tomatoes
in back courtyard privacy,

but you cannot post a letter
choose fresh pasta
pick-up an order from the butcher

make a church visit
browse the bookstore, enjoy a cappuccino
make the daily trip to the grocery market

without heels and pearls.

Beautiful babies are pushed
down the aisle with decorated strollers
by mothers and grandmothers

put together in every way.
They are proud of the new generation
extended family possible

because of their legacy work.
Dressed in the best possible fashion
as men have for years in their cloistered

office space now sprinkled with women,
when outside the home, one must
look like every moment matters.

Raposa

Duomo bell rings once
inhale/inaspirare

Shop doors lock
exhale/aspirare

Walk toward home
inhale/inaspirare

Slice a melon
exhale/aspirare

Water the orchid
inhale/inaspirare

Pour a glass of wine
exhale/aspirare

Get score and headphones
inhale/inaspirare

Settle in listening chair
exhale/aspirare

Remove shoes
inhale/inaspirare

Close eyes
exhale/aspirare

The Gamba

When I turned around
they were bending over the open green case
speaking in hushed tones.

I couldn't bring my stunned self to the edge
to see death or injury.
We were frozen in collective regret.

It was borrowed kindness that was broken
and the heart of the music.

The choir still sang,
hillside Italian church full and unaware
but the firm foundation was missing.

Remaining sadness
was not for the wounded instrument
but for her particular touch.

for Carolyn

GUATEMALA

The Land of Beyond Yet

is not on the maps.

There is no access for
book-bound scholars
or temple thieves.

Guatemalan villagers
and poets
are comfortable drifting
into the unknown.

Ancient Mayan pots
are given away by children
who find them in fields
while carrying water.
Broken pieces
fragments of the past
treasures unearthed
by innocent hands.

This Christmas
ten women and girls
drowned in the lake
taking the Blessed Virgin
on its yearly pilgrimage.
The boat, carved
from one great tree
could not save them.

Exotic colors, flying in twos
at dawn and sunset
screaming to each other
in parrot language
emotionally charge music.
Theirs is the complete vista
above treetops
and unexcavated ruins.

Exposed roots are tangled
in a bed of ferns so textural
eyes cannot remember it.
So many shades of green
intricate designs, when it rains
diamonds and emeralds appear.
Clusters of moist fruit
hang from branches, welcome
food for toucans and sloths.

On the forest floor
a miniature subculture exits.
Carrying bits of vegetation
much larger than themselves
leafcutters move in obedient
lines toward the huge
mound of ants. Do they mourn
hundreds of lives crushed
in one oblivious human step?

Moonlight pours into the Biosphere
reflecting shapes invisible earlier
disorienting even the best guides.
Skin takes on a surreal glow
as howling monkeys play
in this reversed world. It belongs
to them, a land of in-between
of beyond yet.

Lake Peten Itza

floating
on the surface
between earth and sky
weightless
buoyed by human sacrifice
from the deep
soft rain baptizes
my face, my palms
shore voices trail off
my arms outstretched
cruciform
welcoming the heavens
before the storm

Scenes on the road of death

I. In the village

Hover over
the wooden hole
never sit
never

hawk eyes
watch carefully
each stranger

pull the children close

they burned the sacred ceiba
the trunk, the limbs
my cousin's hut
my cousin

the dust left behind
gets in my face
my hair, my teeth
my eyes

it is in the clay oven
that cooks the food
we all eat.

II. The students
The van jerks wildly
to a stop
no place to hide
everyone sees her get sick

we will pretend
to look away, sadness
choking our hearts
collective dread

living things disappeared

clear cut
corn refuses to grow
soil remembers
a different story

roots of giant tress
holding down the underworld
cradling the bones
of our history lesson

the driver is nervous
we cannot travel
this road
at night.

III. Lone bird

It is too quiet
i saw the men come
to make an example
of their brothers and sisters

i saw the bulldozers
scrape the earth of green
to plant red clay
i warned them

my voice was too small

i still sing
in the new field
but no one
answers.

IV. Spirit of the dead

November 1
colorful paper designs
newly painted stones
call me back

a special meal
served with hope
invisible, taken away
like their pain

for a day
the great family
beyond the village
unknown to the young

filled empty lungs
with moist forest air
the first and last breath
repeated.

COSTA RICA

shala

slow barefoot ascent
half-light
incense bids me
marinates golden wood
fills my interior
slips on the breeze
into green canopy beyond

inner and outer touch

a stunning five note song
punctures the silence
alerted
i sink into my mat
close inquiring eyes
mother nature
chants us in

for Janel and Horace
Nexus Institute shala

MEXICO

Copper Canyon Haiku

red fairy duster
cleaning warm Sonora breeze
pleases hummingbirds

      rain and forty-eight
      hours, turn gray thorny branches
      to green desert leaves

a pecan orchard
shades small boys playing with guns
where is the sweetness?

      under dramatic
      clouds, Paquime labyrinth
      ancient city bones

difficult moment
picking thorns from my sandals
i see a rainbow

      only human hair
      his wife's, and bicycle spoke
      the potter's paintbrush

the Aztec people
blossom of the prickly pear
cactus, understood

begging is not bad
her cosmology invites
sharing God's trinkets

carefully placed stones
miles of wall dividing land
families apart

orange and lemon trees
alfresco vision of health
supermarket source

near the cave dwelling
colorful clothes hang drying
on the sun-warmed fence

i smell wood burning
sensuous high mountain crisp
autumn deep breathing

boulder upon rock
suspended mammoth sculpture
mystery balance

empty mission church
altar candles ringing saints
of another time

canyon by moonlight
copper rocks reflecting
my man and myself

       the sea of night stars
       belong to the rich, the poor
       and owls equally

perched halfway between
blue heaven and canyon bed
a bird without wings

       Tarahumara
       people, live in the outdoors
       shelters are for sleep

a huge grasshopper
shared our hacienda room
trapped under a hat

       flower petals float
       in the tiered water fountain
       along with grapefruits

exotic ceiling
up-side-down party flowers
watching as we eat

blink and you will miss
gathering of hummingbirds
delicate food fight

a growing frenzy
inside the hotel courtyard
green conversation

gold and blue with pink
swirling fruit margarita
San Carlos sunset

three women wading
soaking up tropical sun
no thinking allowed

curving away from
cactus hills, dry and sandy
sparkling lagoon

tiny white spirals
gleaming among common stones
nourishing the eye

local prayer practice
lifting the head of a saint
true heart tradition

sacred symbols mix
Jesuit Indigenous
complex histories

      travel companions
      stunning views, shared adventures
      bond between strangers

home to work again
raking gold leaves, crackle swish
travel thoughts fading

about Haiku by Sam Hamill…
*"In three lines totaling seventeen syllables measuring 5-7-5,
a great haiku presents a crystalline moment of image, emotion, and
awareness. Elements of compassion, silence and sense of temporality
often combine to reveal a quality of mystery."*

ENGLAND

looking up

ungendered angels
thrust their chests into the light
wings reaching upward
ready to fly off the cement
pull us up by the shoulders
from hard pews
to hover around the suspended organ
watch the fingers and feet fly
with inspired intention
eyes on the language above the keys
above the words
above the instinct to be appropriate
above the ability for ordinary people
to organize their thoughts
much less their body
to lift sound

Magdalen Green, Oxford

The gardeners
request
that you do not take
shortcuts across the lawns
or play games on the grass
despite
the spell of sunshine.

The grass
is still very easily damaged,
worn patches and scruffs
cannot readily be
made good.
The heavy demands
of summer (including the ball)
are not far away.

UNITED STATES

Blackberry Beach – Orcas Island

An open porch with two handmade chairs face Buck Bay.
Honeysuckle grows in the arbor. Inside, a small wooden table,
crooked switch plates, outlets in weird places, old cabinet
around the sink leans toward the G.E. stove. Drawers are
painted an unusual violet.

The garden has many kinds of flowering plants
comfortable with each other: a butterfly bush with daisies
growing out of it, hydrangea nestled in between rhododendrons,
lavender and snap dragons across the bottom, and a
spectacular rose reaching above it all.

The path to the beach is lined with blackberries and
day lilies. Slippery jagged stones make it difficult to step
down to the tide pool. There are purple star fish. But dead
and dying barnacles stink alongside brown tubular seaweed.
Fancy sailboats drift by looking for the black and white orcas.

"Another fine day" said Marshall, our grey-haired neighbor
just back from gold fields in California with sleeveless tees
and a giant tooth necklace on a chain. He played the guitar
singing, "I love you as much as you love the sea"
the first song he had finished in five years.

We walked to the local restaurant for baked salmon and
blackberry cobbler served with ice cream from a dairy farm.
Giant metal kinetic sculptures, food for our imagination,
were found across the island. A quietly famous artist lives
and works, his property a private exhibit in motion.

The Day Poets Tamed Manhattan

Arriving Penn Station
to harpsichord and strings
unusual soundscape
smell of fresh bagels and coffee
down escalators turned to up
as we approached the taxi queue
everyone stood calmly
agreeably waiting
then driven through
normally frantic streets
even the drag queens
strolling slower
no scurrying briefcases
bumping into each other
at the hotel
no line to check in
attendants noticed us
quiet elevator ride
found our room
and rested.

Later we went to the event
ten poets reading for a friend
sacred elder to them
in the community of living artists
that shape our world
tenderly help us

understand our own lives
and live them more fully
tears flowed at the grace
of the moment in this city
city of violence
noise and competition
we sat at table together
birthday celebration
poets and poet lovers
the Italian waiter
had them sign the menu
he was so glad to serve
jovial famous writers
even the cabbie gave
our loaded car blessings
to end the day.

*The day I accompanied Lucille to the
90th birthday celebration for Stanley Kunitz.*

HUNGARY

Night in Budapest

We enter the small family restaurant
in concert black, carrying our instruments.
He is sitting in the back, a large man
his violin on the table beside him.

Our agent whispers, "You are very lucky,
best band in Budapest, the gypsy king is here."
Hungarian beer and goulash are ordered as
we listen and watch the atmosphere grow.

It is understood, no one would ask him to play
yet, the violin is there, still as his hand
only the slightest gesture speaking worlds
to each player. There are no written scores.

At the end of the meal, he slowly stands as the band
adjusts their positions and become very serious.
The bow touches the string with such intensity,
such character, the whole room pauses.

We are captured. He takes us with him, drawing in
the band one by one as they follow his quick changes
of direction in tempo and mood. My Julliard friends
Jose, Vladimir, and Deborah are moved to tears.

They have just heard all their world-class training
in the first note. As the final startling instruction
the master comes to the table to shake our opened hands.
His is surprisingly soft.

VARIOUS PLACES

Moment in Time ✓

Moravia, in the middle of a huge
field of lettuce
planted in diagonal rows
only one person bends over a hoe.

Budapest, a woman in a navy-blue jacket
prays the stations of the cross, kneeling before each
a small prayerbook with very dark pages
clenched in her hands.

Guatemala, near the Mayan Biosphere Reserve
an elder in a remote village opens
a small museum for ancient shards and pots
unearthed by children, being given to tourists.

Olympic Valley, Lake Tahoe, poets gather in the place
where athletes from around the world walked
by the same bluish-purple clumps of chicory and
watched the sun cut across the rocks to high camp.

St. Mary's City, a student writes about
a gentle street vendor killed in New York City
while his friends on a choir tour bus in Moravia
observe a single farmer in a lettuce field, hoeing.

ST. THOMAS –
U.S. VIRGIN ISLANDS

Island New Year's Eve

The voodoo woman eating fire in the ballroom at midnight
while walking on broken glass would have been enough
when 3 hot pink sprites called enchantments joined her
bending slender double-jointed limbs under and over a limbo bar
to the euphoric beat of a local reggae band, singing about paradise
as 15-foot glittering masked moko jumbies entered the room dancing
their long stilt legs kicking out over seated guests and children.
Invitation to join the conga line found me in a catatonic state
glued to my chair, eyes bulging, head pounding, rum filled.
The clock struck the new year with chaos-colored noise
and I ran out like Cinderella

toward 99 steps leading down to the beach, lit by a true
once-in-a-blue full moon. Gasping at every landing, I passed
scary reflections of variegated palms and tooth-edged cactus
normally ugly iguanas sunning in the moonlight looking wise
manmade resort falls, moist night air softening tension
a large curving shallow pool holding international gossip
the shack of eternal tropical drinks and grilled hamburgers
vacant beach chairs with fragrant sun lotion lingering
to the very edge, glass slippers in hand
phosphorescent wave rim, silent wave after gentle lapping wave
yellow silk soothing an overload of happiness.

KITH AND KIN

Hanging Out the Laundry

for Anne Marie Foley Fryberger

Many years after handing you pins
   from the muslin container with a wire mouth
   standing in the sun by the holly hocks,
I need your help hanging the laundry.

Our third-floor apartment, slightly lower
   than the church bell tower but overlooking
   interwoven clay tile roofs at angles,
has a clothesline on the narrow balcony.

It is a public/private affair, the back courtyard.
   Suddenly, the sizes and shapes of my daily life
   my inner wear particulars
seem wrong to fly before unknown neighbors.

And how do you pin a dress shirt?
   Do you attach it at the shoulders, leaving the arms
   scarecrow swinging or divide complicated seams
in half, making a fold through the stiff collar?

How did you manage to balance the fabric,
   the line, wooden notes clipped on a fresh air staff?
   It seemed easy as I watched you overlapping
garments just enough to make a stronger connection

intentional for our close and growing family.
Holding the empty basket on your slim hip
you walked lightly beyond the clean white wall
my hand clasped in yours, so happy to be useful.

House for Sale

323 Court Street
Mossyrock, Washington
Originally built by pioneer doctor, William Botzer, in 1923

Great family home
Huge kitchen with light-filled breakfast nook
Large dining/living room perfect for potluck dinners
Sunroom for African violets and piano lessons
Large front room window for flock-stenciled Christmas designs or
watching Chevy Malibus cruise by the maple trees
Carpeted staircase for "Mother May I" or "Green Light-Red light"
Monticello wallpaper
Balcony at top of stairs to hide and watch guests arrive
Modern brass push-button light switches
Wide covered front porch for playing outside when it rains,
reading, and having hot chocolate tea parties
Back porch with open storage for all manner of equipment such as
coffee cans needed for hunting garter snakes and
small shovels for making mud pies
Two-car garage for hula-hoop and ping-pong contests
Separate apartment in the basement which can be
rented to local school teachers
Flower gardens for surprising the neighbors on May Day
Laurel bushes for making victory crowns
Blooming Hawthorne tree, branches perfect for prom and graduation
Holly for Christmas wreaths
Pink Camelia bush for decorating Mother's Day cakes

Italian plums for eating
Giant maple leaves for tracing and making piles
in which to jump before burning
Dandelions for checking to see if someone likes butter
Windowed attic to store treasures and play dress-up
Biking distance to the lake, short walk to school
Vintage swing set
Close hike up Mossyrock hill for a view of the valley
Blackberry bush hallows to hold secret club meetings

Memory equity you earn is yours
Over time it will only increase in value.

Anniversary Song

The large mirrored dressing table
on the second floor of my grandparent's brownstone
in the Irish section of Anaconda, Montana
was low enough for my sister and me to reach.
When nobody was watching
we would sneak into their bedroom
to touch the jewelry and perfume bottles.

In the closet we found hexagon boxes with exotic hats
handed down from her wealthy aunt in Chicago.
We tried them on, muffling giggles, then
carefully returned them to their perfect containers.

But the most exciting and risky secret moment
was the discovery of the small blue round box
filled with sweet-smelling face powder
and a soft pink puff.

Lifting the golden knob on the lid
we were thrilled and terrified to hear
a mysterious tune winding into itself, repeating
and repeating, exposing our illicit adventure
now curiously locked in our memory
like the anniversaries, we later learned
this love song was marking.

He Sings

He sings. He has known power.
He has held his own baby in his large hands.
He has painted music with a choir.

He is walking
toward the double glass doors of a theater
from a dark engaging film
out into the real world.

He wants to breathe unconditioned air.
He wants to filter random street noise
with his trained ear.

Perhaps he wants to lose his way
for an undetermined time.
He is no longer in charge of the rookery.

for Larry
end of being provost, SMCM
Spring 2011

Rice Cereal

I added pear water

first flakes of

worldly nourishment

mixed with

pure sweetness

mother's milk

genetically matched

for wholeness.

Precious Jewelry

I. He found an old watch
    took it apart
    insides glistening
    miniature movements
    strong in form
    intentional design.

    Removing one screw
    a perfect space appeared
    for a silver chain.
    It came to me
    in a used golden box.

II. Bright red string
    connecting colorful beads
    wooden and glass
    shapes of joy
    touching
    with confident affection.

    This happy chaos
    brings strength
    endless companions
    grounded
    in freedom.

III. A slice of walnut
    brown courage
    spiraling
    circular insides of God's fruit
    hand-polished to shine
    though energy and innocence
    need no refinement.

    Given with love
    illuminated by imagination
    how could the song from that tree
    have known its own beauty?

for Micah, Dominic, and Olivia

Adam's Kiss

It is for all of us
this moment of truth
this step out of earth time
when, waiting at the school bus stop
we say "you are loved"
just in case.

Collective fears surface;
school shootings
needless competition
personal cruelties.

The bus appears
and there is a scramble to board.
I want to say something,
"I am sorry I hurried you
life is too fast and too short
it doesn't matter
what matters is…."

Then I see it, Adam's kiss.

Our permission to go to work
leaving our children behind
letting them face the day
alone
but loved.

Flashlight Tag

warm summer nights
call fireflies
a million random light points
glittering

three-dimensional fields
counterpoint stars
the dark space in-between
no assistance from the moon

cautious children, running
holding their own lights
household variety
battery dependent

this neighborhood game
invented and policed
without adults
one must know the land

bumps, dips, and ditches
once Mariel, new to the area
ran straight through
Edna's garden, the rose bush

slicing her legs
preserving the secret
of her location
she held a stinging silence

Dom got antibiotic
but the salve
of friendship
was a stronger fix

Sixteen

Olivia, your lifeguard brown body
Is getting stronger every day

I am amazed at your muscular legs
Wearing boys lacrosse shorts

Deep red tank tops
Gliding over your courage

You do not yet have any idea, the grace
Contained in that six-foot frame.

When you stepped in the skimmer
And gashed your shin, I felt it

I held you close, stitched leg throbbing
And talked about ordinary healers

A litany of common friends poured out
Making us feel better, suspending

Momentarily, the awkward tension
Sometimes pain, of being fully human.

Bluebird, Redbird, Songbird

A small nest is perched on a bluff
above the river. Ospreys and eagles
mark the territory, but real authority
is held by the ancient heron.

Loons gather, noticing the shaking nest
wanting to be the first to know.
Gossips by design, they get half the story
As they dive and appear in unexpected places.

The first egg broke. It was a blue jay.
Quickly with confidence he stepped to the edge
"I like this, when can I fly across the river?

Another egg opened, to everyone's surprise
it was a cardinal. "A red bird in a
blue nest," he said, and began to study.

Soon enough the last egg cracked.
"Get me out of here," she sang. Though smaller
she began to organize them in lydian mode.

Parents usually get food separately
while one tends the nest. Too much alike,
these guardians fly everywhere together, and now
they watch with amazement.

One said to the other, "What do you think
we should do?" They steadied themselves
against a giant oak, as the three
flew on the wind in different directions.

*Written for the recital given by Olivia upon her high school graduation,
the same year that Dominic graduated from St. Mary's College of Mary-
land and Micah graduated from University of Virginia. 2002*

Home Wish

I wish this home to be a gathering place for solace.

A place to undress high personal expectations
confusion of purpose
sting of betrayal
messages unanswered
and wishful-thinking list of good deeds
while gazing at the river.

I wish this space to conjure laughter.

Humor percolating from ordinary living
overshadowed by thick schedules
group humor, like support
reflected off shared stories
illuminating what was lost in the responsibility
of being adult in a serious world.

I wish visitors and family to feel the long arms
of unconditional acceptance.

When leaving our space, they would feel heard
wrapped in possibility
yet the calm of being enough
touched by beauty,
determined by their own eyes and
hold an inside smile that doesn't show on the face.

Spring Cleaning

My new rake
has steel tongs.

On Saturday,
as I ripped
through tangled ivy
discovering daffodils

clawed the forest floor
unfolding layers of wet leaves
exposing insects

jerked dead limbs
away from the house
flinging them toward the ravine

my winter body said,
this   feels   good.

banishing demons

stay away from my daughter
you demons of doubt

it doesn't matter if you visit
every artist in the universe, driven

to put body and soul on the line
this singer is off limits

her work ethic fierce
commitment total

do not take advantage
of the natural inclination

to be thrilled by the
perfect turn of a phrase or
complex sotto voce moment

beware

she will crush you
with the rage in courage

never to collect the pieces
of your useless intent

you are no match
for this kind of beauty

Justin

Standing in silence, so close to Julia
we could trace the curve of her hip.
Tulip poplars, right angle branches extended
arms locked, steadying the
strong oak in the middle
determined to see the body
with her own eyes, yet
blue and red flashing continued
cutting dusk into pieces
of rescue squad static.

Julia and Robin were led to the river
parents only.
We followed them, holding hands
like children
flashlights at our feet
through swamp grass and periwinkles
toward the lullabies.

After the last hymn
all processed to church point
for the internment.
Though the bell-ringer
could not see the pond
bells peeled
just as Julia put her hand into
the ashes, rubbing the same flesh
that came from her body
into her face, forever.

Deeply Rooted

When first you sprouted in Ann Arbor and Purcellville,
adoring parents and grandparents tended each garden.
Delight filled their eyes and spilled over, adding much
needed moisture. They fed you miracle gro of foreign
lands, your Amsterdam and Paris playgrounds forming
ultra rich soil for a strong wondrous root system.

Sibling plants shared the special landscapes adding
color and companionship, reflecting genus and species.
You learned to lean into the wind during storms
then turn toward the sun for strength
while parents and grandparents joyfully watched.

One day you were independently replanted in a new
Arlington garden. You noticed each other.
You recognized something familiar and thrilling.
Stems became vines, growing better together
than apart, as in a particular Nebbiolo hillside light.

Today parents, friends, relatives living and not,
witness the grafting of your two uniquely beautiful
strains, grown with the same careful tenderness
the same love that will continue in all ways, always.

for Anna and Micah
Veritas Vineyards
Afton, Virginia
10/24/09

Q Street

Saturday, I walked into a poem. There were signs.

Instead of rigidly placed matching bushes, textural herbs were roughly cut
for their true kitchen use, and I do believe I saw the white trumpet
of Jimson Weed, favorite of Georgia O'Keefe, right at the steps.

The entry must have been glass as the wide hall with brass mailboxes
was flooded with light, or perhaps kindness herself had opened the door.

A black iron handrail guided me up the stairs, and up, and up. I was lifted
to another landing full of light, with a mirror to remind me it was me.

I walked through door #307, and I discovered the tree house.
Perched in the top branches of an elderly oak, tree of doors or gateway
between worlds in Celtic tradition, there was a perfect dwelling place
for two and two. Two people, two cats.

There was music of course, and colorful art on old walls newly painted.
I walked to the middle, the inner so close to the outer, sat down
sinking into the green sofa. I heard the soft pop of real cork leaving
a handpicked bottle, as a pungent red bouquet filled the room.

In almost every direction I saw book spines. Mottled vertical lines
charged with ideas and stories. Curiosity made into objects.

Two platoons of purple and gold soldiers peeping in the windows
guarded the space. On a peaceful mission, they kept a smiling vigilance.

A carved wooden sewing machine case held family photos and
fresh cut flowers in a fluted heirloom vase reigned over all.

Not a static container, this house was more like a living sieve through
which people pass each day. It had the feel of connection and respect,
the hard work of paying attention. Exciting shared adventures
were revealed as the potential for more was palpable.

Even when the leaves surrounding this tree house fall into winter,
bare long-armed branches will affectionately enfold the precious contents.

for Dominic and Danielle

No Words Required

outrageous laughter
sparkling eye roll   for love

thin martini lip, lemon
twist held by silver geese   for love

stew pot on the stove
fragrance of tenderness   for love

wild heart dancing
chasing away small sorrows   for love

lapiz lazuli wall built
scaffold of a shared life   for love

emerald light bathes
a handmade painting desk   for love

gift for the singer, while
sheltering dreams   for love

cold center city train
end of day warm embrace   for love

for love   for love

evermore

for Augusto and Olivia
May 31, 2020

Violet

Just as we were viewing a contemporary condo
beside NPR offices, floor to ceiling windows,
community gardens, indoor pool and parking,
near an organic market, bakery, library, theater,
and a cinema down the street....

my husband bought me a bike.

Not an urban ride with a cute basket
and chain guard (which I secretly desired)
no, a Diamondback hybrid with a solid frame
a long coast, and gears as smooth as butter.

I quickly fell for the strength and deep color,
an invitation. Maybe we have some years
breathing country air, before living inside the
beltway with famous cultural enrichment venues
and historical monuments. Wind in the face
childhood memories of a long ride have
currently captured my imagination.

Untethered

Today we step forward
remove redundancy
reduce cost.

It began in a winterized beach house
rainbow mailbox
paused on Amsterdam sabbatical

moved near a good elementary school
built a small house
came to rest on the river.

Connecting our east coast life
to our west coast family
before the lure of digital

no longer named in the community book
access denied, disconnected
a 32-year-old number, 301-862-9133

the landline is removed.

Message to Shirley

Like you
she is fierce.
You raised strong daughters.
When the accident occurred
the collective will of three
extraordinary performing families
gathered to fight for her breath.

Like you
her virtuoso fingers
wrap around an instrument
her man, and her children
with equal intensity and wisdom.
If music is the family lifeblood
then love is the connecting tissue.

Like you
her soft face has mischievous eyes
the flirting glance at her beloved
accompanied by a giggle
that changed but never left.
His affectionate teasing
hiding desperate proximity to loss,
provided solid ground.

She saw you in the hospital,
thank you for answering.

for Debbie

Three Stones

Rain becoming ice. Store windows glazing.
We are losing our footing. More slippery sidewalk.
Harry's Tap Room. Fireplace glowing, glasses lifted.

Warm people, smartly dressed. Too many.
Moving about closely. Cool quick pardons offered.
Engaged noise. Bouncing off rich dark wood.

Colorful designer tile adds conversation. Surface talk.
Observing eyes. Reaching beyond companions.
All wish to connect. Longing for more than fun.

She reaches into a small purse. Three stones from Seattle.
Northwest memory. Smooth shapes that sparkle under water.
My hand wraps around her gift. Something solid, something real.

river night

a small red boat
sits offshore, alone
waiting

one full moon
a sparkling light path
cuts across dark water

iridescent sails lift
music of a million wings
warm, golden unfamiliar sounds
random as fireflies

oysters slowly open
hidden crabs surface
great blues and snowy white egrets
line the beach

the sailor appears
skin luminous, moving
with perfect precision
heart visible

soft scent breathing
winter jasmine, spring honeysuckle
summer lavender
autumn forget-me-nots

calm winds and following seas
my love, embrace
the long arms of the moon

The Dinner

Paint on the curved steps is cracked,
the screen door has driveway dust.
Behind is a rainforest.

Called by increasing aromas
and curiosity toward the kitchen,
time evaporates from steaming pots.

Daylight filters softly against the eye
of peacock feathers, earth-colored books,
clay shapes containing shells and stones,

a glass sphere, drawings and paintings
by friends, for friends, with friends.
Complicated and engaging space

inviting opinions, colorful garden meal,
people laughing, talking, listening,
playing, tasting, pouring, then leaving

refreshed.

for Andrea

Eliza at the Piano

Red chiffon tied in satin at the wrist
roses and lotus flowers floating
as proper presentation
turns provocative.

Black lacquered lid reflecting focus
lips slightly open, relaxed cheeks and neck
a hungry tiger charging
while a low chiming bell is suspended.

Old soul fingers
and elegant expressive hands
lift freshly wrought stories
into this unbounded space.

Her key devotion
artistry
contains intricate inlaid patterns
human, mellifluous.

Noble simplicity of sound
perfectly strained surface tension
enter the organs of my body
to a depth surgeons cannot reach.

Love Indeed

Love Indeed. Love and memory.
Love and memory and a heart pumping from
images of new works seen on this machine.
Friends and art and babies feeding goats
eating lilacs while sweet red peppers roasting
fresh as the day they were painted.
Then to walk off the known path
encountering obscure frescoes sublime
house of handmade furniture, still life everywhere
particular color yes colorful lively conversations
drifting into hillside gardens. Harpsichord playing
woman, letter in one hand, blue ribbon in the other
is wondering what mystery of gratitude
will next appear.

for Alan and Lani

Sursum Corda – Hearts Lifted

that you should cup the tears
and fly them past the darkly carved gate
in the exquisite arc of your
conducting hand
beyond stained glass saints
through the rose blue glow
sliding past pillar walls
gathering up even the fearful souls
in the back
and fly out the great green opening
at the end of the manmade sacred space
into your new construction
never alone
never without love

for Bruce Neswick,
last evensong at the National Cathedral

Millie

Sitting in the back pew
between a bishop and a soldier
furiously crocheting
the resurrection color
you spoke to me, from your
peaceful half-opened bed.

It's like the time
you and the children
walked down Bauer Road
after the ice storm
all cold and worried
about me, to find
the fireplace crackling
a home-canned meal
ready to share.

My prayer-reciting lips
began to taste the last cantaloupe
sweetest, from a dry summer
you plucked from your garden
and delivered to the door
of our new home.

Saffron Rice

Ruby red stigma of the crocus
three fragile stems
plucked
from the purple flower
rare beauty.

Saffron released
cooked with rice and raisins
on another continent
regal heat
rich golden warmth.

Delicious friendship
humor spiced conversations
white gardenias and
kindness
suddenly missing

like the big-bellied cat
from kitchen light
colorful family feast table
suspended
familiar chair of grace.

Now quietly tasting
extraordinary
capacity for love
while Burmese dancers
continue to watch over us.

for Ohnmar

Saying Goodbye

We closed the panels of the mirror
Bringing the river into our bedroom
Shimmering the ceiling
Turning the fresh air orange at sunset
Full moon beams reflecting to our house.

The north window looks into the canopy
Of a large Japanese Maple
Set like a gem in an old growth forest.
Embroidered gold silk frames the view.
In December the neighbor's fantasy
Christmas lights peek through.

French doors guard an empty walk-in closet
That housed a glaring abundance.
Ample space for a person without a home.

A tiny bathroom looms large
Natural light, wainscotting walls
Topped with delphinium blue
The soft white terry shower curtain
Protects a bubbling spa tub, ironically
Too loud to enjoy.

Tomorrow morning a technician comes
To disassemble the bed.
It is our last night here.

Harmonica

This harp can hide
in a deep pocket
until the solitary moment
when quiet is too much
your heart, torn into pieces
by war revisited
wisdom unwanted.

The smooth metal on your side
is no longer a gun.

Small sound in the wilderness
of human nature distorted
this reminder, victory of spirit
blessing of family and friends
who need you,
your words, your memories
to protect us.

for Wayne and all Veterans

Lu

There you are in Barnes and Noble
Lucille Clifton
sitting between Chaucer and Coleridge
The Book of Light
 familiar phrases speaking
pain and vision, splendor and fury
while all I can think
is girlfriend.

You heal the public
with personal accounts of loss
powerful lines
yet laced with humor
difficult human truths
luminous   dazzling
tossed with
evidence of survival.

After dinner one evening
Kathy and I sat close
so very thankful
your latest victory over cancer
still settling
I held your silicone replacement
in the breathless palm
of my hand.

It felt soft and warm
as the cheek
of a wise woman.

Under the Weeping Willow

A slight woman, Irish beauty
is clutching her balance
and his photograph
full of laughter
handsome Air Corps stories
her piano man
on the first anniversary
of his birth, without him.

She is leaning in a new
direction, his shoulder so real
though not visible to us
like a slight breeze
through bare willow branches.

The corners of her
youthful red lips
are beginning to lift.

for Mom

"For poems are not words, after all, but fires for the cold, ropes let down to the lost, something as necessary as bread in the pockets of the hungry."

—Mary Oliver
A Poetry Handbook

Author in 1983
Photo credit, Jimo Perini
used by permission of Helene Perini